T0400518

About This Book

Title: *Sell It!*

Step: 1

Word Count: 102

Skills in Focus: All short vowels

Tricky Words: buy, things, shops, pay, with, people, what, cars, have

Ideas For Using This Book

Before Reading:

- **Comprehension:** Look at the title and cover image together. Ask readers what they know about buying and selling. What new things do they think they might learn in this book?
- **Accuracy:** Practice saying the tricky words listed on page 1.
- **Phonemic Awareness:** Have readers point to the word *sell* in the title. Practice taking apart and putting together the sounds. Ask readers to tap a new finger to their thumb to count the sounds they hear. Ask: How many sounds are in the word *sell*? What is the first sound? Middle sound? Ending sound? Change the /s/ to /b/. What word is it? Repeat with the word *well*. Change the /w/ to /f/. Ask students to name other -*ell* words they know.

During Reading:

- Have readers point under each word as they read it.
- **Decoding:** If readers are stuck on a word, help them say each sound and blend the sounds together smoothly. Be sure to point out any short vowel sounds.
- **Comprehension:** Invite students to talk about what new things they are learning about buying and selling while reading. What are they learning that they didn't know before?

After Reading:

Discuss the book. Some ideas for questions:

- Have you ever bought something? What did you buy?
- Have you ever sold something? What did you sell?

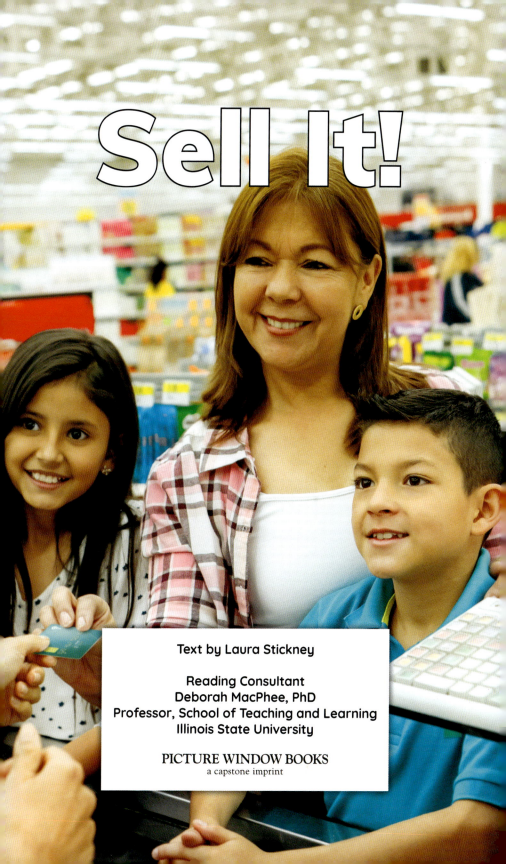

Sell It!

Text by Laura Stickney

Reading Consultant
Deborah MacPhee, PhD
Professor, School of Teaching and Learning
Illinois State University

PICTURE WINDOW BOOKS
a capstone imprint

Kids can buy lots of things.
Kids can sell things.

A kid has hot rod cars.

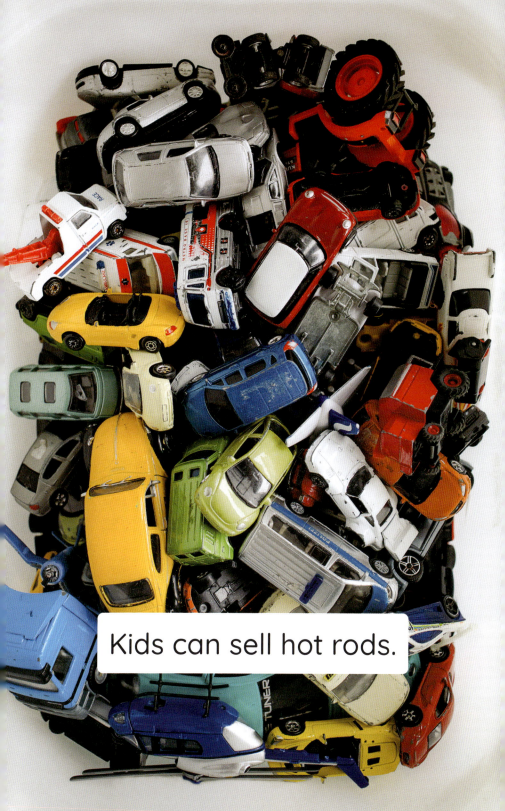

Kids can sell hot rods.

Kids can have hats.

Kids can sell hats.

Kids sell to get bills.

Kids can get things with bills.

At shops, kids can pick up cans.

Kids can get pens.
Kids can get caps.

Add up the sum.
Pay with bills.

Pack cans in bags.
Put caps in sacks.

People can get jobs in shops.

Shops can sell bags or sun hats.

Get a hat. Cut off its tags.
Put it on. Pack it up.

20

Let's sell!
What will sell well?

More Ideas:

Phonemic Awareness Activity

Practicing Short Vowels:

Say a short vowel story word for readers to practice segmenting the sounds. Tell readers to hop in place as they break apart the word, hopping once for each sound. Begin with *sell*. They will hop once for /s/, again for /e/, and once more for /ll/. What sound was first? What is the middle sound? Ending sound? Optional: Readers can clap or tap for each sound.

Suggested words:
• well
• hat
• bill
• tag
• sum

Extended Learning Activity

Play Pretend:

Ask readers to imagine that they have a job at a shop. Help them set up an imaginary shop with furniture or toys. Then have them collect items around them that their shop can sell. Pretend to buy and sell the items at the shop. Take turns having the reader be the buyer and seller. Challenge students to use words with short vowel sounds during the game.

Published by Picture Window Books, an imprint of Capstone
1710 Roe Crest Drive, North Mankato, Minnesota 56003
capstonepub.com

Copyright © 2026 by Capstone.
All rights reserved. No part of this publication may be reproduced
in whole or in part, or stored in a retrieval system, or transmitted in
any form or by any means, electronic, mechanical, photocopying,
recording, or otherwise, without written permission of the publisher.

Library of Congress Cataloging-in-Publication Data is available
on the Library of Congress website.

ISBN: 9798875226977 (hardback)
ISBN: 9798875229343 (paperback)
ISBN: 9798875229329 (eBook PDF)

Image Credits: iStock: Caiaimage/Paul Bradbury, 22–23,
Drazen Zigic, 16, Hispanolistic, 2–3, jonathansloane, 9, lissart, 8,
NRuedlsueli, 7, SDI Productions, 11, xavierarnau, 14–15; Shutterstock:
arrowsmith2, 13, Debbie Ann Powell, 18–19, Littlekidmoment, 12,
Miridda, 20–21, New Africa, cover, paulaphoto, 1, 10, PeopleImages.
com/Yuri A, 6, 24, stockfour, 4–5, Tanya_Terekhina, 17

Printed and bound in China. PO 6274